# BREATH OF HEAVEN

AMY GRANT

ISBN 0-8499-1732-8

Printed in the United States of America

0 1 2 3 4 WOR 9 8 7 6 5 4 3 2 1

"Breath of Heaven (Mary's Song)" Written by Amy Grant & Chris Eaton © 1992 Age to Age Music, Inc. (ASCAP)(Admin. By The Loving Company) / Clouseau Music, Ltd. (PRS)(Admin. By Bug Music) All Rights Reserved. Used By Permission

"The Road To Bethlehem" Written by Amy Grant & Beverly Darnall
Cover & Interior Design: Susan Browne; Susan Browne Design
Images in photo composites © Photodisc, © EyeWire/PictureNow.com, © Jimmy Abegg, © The Doré Bible Illustrations

W PUBLISHING GROUP™
www.wpublishinggroup.com
A Division of Thomas Nelson, Inc.
www.ThomasNelson.com

CCM
BOOKS

# BREATH OF HEAVEN

# FOREWORD

*Amy Grant*

*It was the early* It was the early fall of 1989.
Two friends and I made plans for an autumn trip to the
woods … a much needed road trip to a cabin in Indiana. We all
had children at home; two of us were pregnant at the time
and looking forward to long, uninterrupted talks by the fire.
I don't remember much about the first night. Over ten years
have passed since then. But I'll never forget the next day.

The conversation started with our first cup of coffee and by late afternoon we were still talking, and still in our bathrobes. Most people have life experiences that remain untold—secret tragedies. Maybe it was the safety of the cabin, the fact that the phone never rang that enabled our friend to tell her story. I'm not going to recount that story here. I can't say anything without saying too much. In the event that she should ever pick up this book, it is important to me that she knows that the safety she felt all those years ago is still in place. What I can say is that she told us a story that was sobering and terrifying.

I was seven months into my pregnancy, carrying my first daughter. Listening to this woman's story, I felt for the first time a very real fear for what might happen, what *could* happen to my child, despite all of my efforts to keep her safe. I guess I was more sheltered than I had imagined.

A little bit of evil goes a long way.

A big dose is devastating.

A LITTLE BIT OF EVIL

GOES A LONG WAY.

A BIG DOSE IS DEVASTATING.

I COULD NOT MAKE

ANY SENSE OF LIFE,

AT LEAST NOT

OF THAT WOMAN'S LIFE.

———————————————————————

We took a break in our conversation as a result of emotional fatigue as much as anything. The sun would be setting soon and we all needed a little space to digest everything that had been spoken. I showered and dressed and went outside. I wanted to cry. I wanted to yell at someone. Instead, I picked my way down the wooded hill and crossed a creek by crawling on my hands and knees over a fallen tree.

I could not make any sense of life, at least not of that woman's life. *Where was God? Where is there any peace to be found?* I could not find any inside of me.

In the midst of all of my anxiousness, I looked up and saw a deer standing in the trees about 30 feet away from me. It was not much bigger than a fawn, though it was old enough to have lost its spots. Distracted from my thoughts, I started walking slowly toward the deer. It did not run. When I was just a few feet away I got down on my knees and continued to move toward it. I was close enough to touch it.

Slowly I stretched out my hand until I touched the deer on the nose. We both jumped back a little. Still, it did not run. Again I reached out. This time I touched the fur on its neck… then its shoulder. I was petting it ever so gently… scratching its chest until I found myself wrapping my arms around its neck and crying. It was the most peaceful interaction I have ever had with an animal. After awhile I slowly backed away, turned and walked to the creek. When I turned back, the deer was gone.

I was so amazed…so filled with wonder. It's hard to put into words the comfort I drew from such an unexpected experience. I felt a renewed sense of hope.

The next day, as we were packing to leave, the owner of the cabin dropped by to see us off. I asked her how long they had been feeding the deer around there. She thought about it a minute and said "I can't say that I've ever seen a deer here before."

"Peace I leave with you, My peace I give you … Let not your heart be troubled, neither let it be afraid." John 14:27

"PEACE I LEAVE WITH YOU,

MY PEACE I GIVE YOU...

LET NOT YOUR HEART

BE TROUBLED,

NEITHER LET IT BE AFRAID."

JOHN 14:27

THE PRINCE OF PEACE

WAS BORN IN A STABLE.

HE WAS SENT TO

BIND UP BROKEN HEARTS.

"Blessed be the God and Father of our Lord Jesus Christ, the Father of mercies and God of all comfort, who comforts us in all our tribulation, that we may be able to comfort those who are in any trouble, with the comfort with which we ourselves are comforted by God." 2 Corinthians 1:3-4

Comfort comes from unexpected places.

The Prince of Peace was born in a stable. He was sent to bind up broken hearts. Many of us have been surprised by mercy and forever changed by it. It comes often in stillness. Sometimes it comes in a song.

I have been told on more than one occasion that the words to this song have been a source of strength and hope during a dark time.

*"…I am frightened by the load I bear…"*
*"…Must I walk this path alone?"*
*"Breath of Heaven, hold me together…"*

This song is a prayer. It is a prayer that fits a lot of people's circumstances because it is a cry for mercy. Some nights on stage I can hardly get through the song for knowing all of the collective, unspoken pain of the lives in front of me. And so, the words become my prayer for the listener, and the reader, as well as the singer.

*Amy Grant*

THIS SONG IS A PRAYER.

IT IS A PRAYER THAT

FITS A LOT OF PEOPLE'S

CIRCUMSTANCES

BECAUSE IT IS A

CRY FOR MERCY.

# THE ROAD TO

That night, Mary found herself in completely unfamiliar territory. She didn't recognize this place or this road, didn't even recognize her own body.

Shifting her weight once again on the back of the donkey, she readjusted the bulk of her belly. The rhythm of Joseph's footfall, the endless shuffling of hooves on the dusty road might have been enough to hypnotize her, if it weren't for this overwhelming discomfort. Impossible to sleep, impossible to rest. Impossible to

# BETHLEHEM

even explain this situation. She had endured the sly glances from the boys in her village, had been pained by the way the girls avoided her. And now, far from home and far from the comfort of her own mother's wisdom and experience, she faces her destiny alone. Over and over she remembers the words of the angel: "Nothing is impossible with God." She knows. This is no mistake. He called her by name.

I HAVE TRAVELED MANY MOONLESS NIGHTS COLD

# AND WEARY

with a babe inside

And having come in the angel said to her, Rejoice, highly favored

When she saw him, she was troubled at his saying, and considered what

be afraid, Mary, for you have found favor with God. And behold, you

call His name Jesus. He will be great, and will be called the Son

of His father David. And He will reign over the house of Jacob for

AND I WONDER WHAT I'VE DONE

HOLY FATHER YOU HAVE COME

AND CHOSEN ME NOW

TO CARRY YOUR SON

I AM

WAITING

IN A

SILENT

PRAYER

IN A
WORLD
AS COLD AS
STONE

*must i walk*

'is path alone

MUST I WALK THIS PATH ALONE

Be with me now

BE WITH ME NOW

# BREATH

## *of* HEA

### *Hold*

VEN

*me together*

BREATH OF HEAVEN

BREATH OF HEAVEN

lighten

MY DARKNESS

# POUR OVER ME

YOUR HOLINESS

# FOR YOU ARE HOLY

BREATH OF HEAVEN

DO YOU
WONDER

AS YOU
WATCH
MY FACE

IF A WISER ONE

SHOULD HAVE

HAD MY PLACE

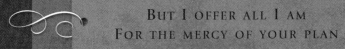

BUT I OFFER ALL I AM
FOR THE MERCY OF YOUR PLAN

# HELP ME
# BE STRONG

# HELP ME
# BE

HELP ME

# BREATH OF HEAVEN

BREATH OF HEAVEN

HOLD ME TOGETHER

BE FOREVER NEAR ME

BREATH OF HEAVEN


BREATH OF HEAVEN

LIGHTEN MY DARKNESS

POUR OVER ME YOUR HOLINESS

FOR YOU ARE HOLY

BREATH OF HEAVEN

THE PEOPLE WHO WALKED IN DARKNESS

HAVE SEEN A GREAT LIGHT;

THOSE WHO DWELT IN
THE LAND OF THE SHADOW OF DEATH,

UPON THEM A LIGHT HAS SHINED.

For unto us a Child is born,

Unto us a Son is given;

And the government will be upon His shoulder,

And His name will be called

Wonderful, Counselor, Mighty God,

Everlasting Father, Prince of Peace.

Of the increase of His government and peace

There will be no end,

Upon the throne of David and over His kingdom,

To order it and establish it with judgement and justice

From that time forward, even forever.

The zeal of the Lord of hosts will perform this.

ISAIAH 9:2, 6-7

*Now in the sixth month the angel Gabriel was sent by God to a city of Galilee named Nazareth, to a virgin betrothed to a man whose name was Joseph, of the house of David. The virgin's name was Mary. And having come in, the angel said to her, "Rejoice, highly favored one, the Lord is with you; blessed are you among women!"*

But when she saw him she was troubled at his saying, and considered what manner of greeting this was. Then the angel said to her, "Do not be afraid, Mary, for you have found favor with God. And behold, you will conceive in your womb and bring forth a Son, and shall call His name Jesus. He will be great and will be called the Son of the Highest and the Lord God will give Him the throne of His father David. And He will reign over the house of Jacob forever, and of His kingdom there will be no end."

Then Mary said to the angel, "How can this be, since I do not know a man?" And the angel answered and said to her, "The Holy Spirit will come upon you, and the power of the Highest will overshadow you; therefore, also, that Holy One who is to be born will be called the Son of God. Now indeed, Elizabeth your relative has also conceived a son in her old age; and this is now the sixth month for her who was called barren. For with God nothing will be impossible." Then Mary said, "Behold the maidservant of the Lord! Let it be to me according to your word." And the angel departed from her.

LUKE 1:26-38

And Mary said: "My soul magnifies the Lord,
And my spirit has rejoiced in God my Savior.
For He has regarded the lowly state of His maidservant;
For behold, henceforth all generations will call me blessed.
For He who is mighty has done great things for me,
And holy is His name,

And His mercy is on those who fear Him

From generation to generation.

He has shown strength with His arm;

He has scattered the proud in the imagination of their hearts.

He has put down the mighty from their thrones,

And exalted the lowly.

He has filled the hungry with good things,

And the rich He has sent away empty.

He has helped His servant Israel,

In remembrance of His mercy,

As He spoke to our fathers,

To Abraham and to his seed forever."

LUKE 1:46-55

# FILLING THE WORLD

HE LIES IN A MANGER.

—*Augustine*

*This book is dedicated with love to
Cindy and Michael Parseghian and their children,
Ara, Marcia, and Christa.*